A Rookie reader®

Family Photo

Written by Dana Meachen Rau
Illustrated by Mike Gordon

Children's Press®
A Division of Scholastic Inc.
New York • Toronto • London • Auckland • Sydney
Mexico City • New Delhi • Hong Kong
Danbury, Connecticut

For Charlie and Allison, who can never sit still!
—D. R.

To Doodie, who appreciates my art!
—M. G.

Reading Consultant

Cecilia Minden-Cupp, PhD
Former Director of the Language and Literacy Program
Harvard Graduate School of Education
Cambridge, Massachusetts

Cover Design: The Design Lab
Interior Design: Herman Adler

Library of Congress Cataloging-in-Publication Data

Rau, Dana Meachen, 1971–
Family photo / by Dana Meachen Rau ; illustrated by Mike Gordon.
p. cm. — (A rookie reader)
ISBN-10: 0-531-12469-X (lib. bdg.) 0-531-12492-4 (pbk.)
ISBN-13: 978-0-531-12469-7 (lib. bdg.) 978-0-531-12492-5 (pbk.)
1. English language—Prepositions—Juvenile literature. I. Gordon, Mike, ill. II. Title. III. Series.
PE1335.R38 2006
428.2–dc22 2006007597

1 2 3 4 5 6 7 8 9 10 R 16 15 14 13 12 11 10 09 08 07

Grandpa, stand in the grass.

Grandma, sit on this chair.

Uncle Joe, stand by the table.

Aunt Sue can stand over there.

Mom can sit beside Grandpa.

Brother can sit on her lap.

Dad can stand with the baby.
Someone wake up Spot from his nap.

Big sister, stand on the left.
Little sister, stand on the right.

Hurry, everyone! Please stay still.
We can't do this all night!

Cousins, crowd close together.
I still can't see you all!

Tom, get onto Bob's shoulders.
Be careful not to fall!

Jack, stand behind Bob.
We don't have a moment to spare!

Sally, come on over!
Can you kneel over there?

I think I can see Cousin Fred if he hangs upside down from that tree.

Now everyone take out your cameras,
and take a picture of me!

Word List (95 words)

(Words in **bold** are prepositions.)

a	come	his	**on**	table
all	cousin	hurry	**onto**	take
and	cousins	I	**out**	that
aunt	crowd	if	**over**	the
baby	dad	**in**	picture	there
be	do	Jack	please	think
behind	don't	Joe	right	this
beside	everyone	kneel	Sally	**to**
big	fall	lap	see	together
Bob	Fred	left	shoulders	Tom
Bob's	**from**	little	sister	tree
brother	get	me	sit	uncle
by	grandma	mom	someone	**up**
cameras	grandpa	moment	spare	upside down
can	grass	nap	Spot	wake
can't	hangs	night	stand	we
careful	have	not	stay	**with**
chair	he	now	still	you
close	her	**of**	Sue	your

About the Author

Dana Meachen Rau loves to get together with her family. When she's not trying to get everyone to sit still to take a picture, she is writing children's books. Dana has written more than 150 books, including early readers and nonfiction. She lives with her family in Burlington, Connecticut.

About the Illustrator

Mike Gordon was born in Lancashire England. In 1993, he moved to Santa Barbara, California, with his four kids. He still lives there and continues to scribble his way through books with the help of his wife, two kitties, and plenty of chocolate chip cookies.